CONTINENTS IN CLOSE-UP

EUROPE

MALCOLM PORTER and KEITH LYE

RAINTREE
STECK-VAUGHN
PUBLISHERS
RSVP ®

A Cherrytree Book
Designed and produced by
AS Publishing
Text by Keith Lye
Illustrated by Malcolm Porter and Raymond Turvey

First published 2001
by Cherrytree Press

First published in the United States 2002
by Raintree Steck-Vaughn Publishers

Library of Congress Cataloguing in Publication Data

Porter, Malcolm
  Europe. - (Continents in close-up)
  1.Children's atlases
  2.Europe - Maps for children
  I.Title II.Lye, Keith
  912.4

ISBN 0-7398-3241-7

Printed in Hong Kong

CONTINENTS IN CLOSE-UP

EUROPE

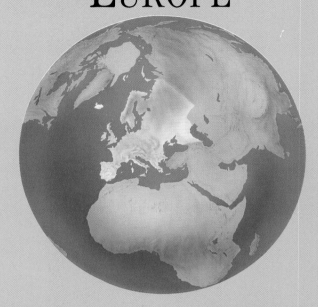

This illustrated atlas combines maps, pictures, flags, globes, information panels, diagrams, and charts to give an overview of the whole continent, and a closer look at each of its countries and at the Atlantic and Arctic oceans.

COUNTRY CLOSE-UPS

Each double-page spread has these features:

Introduction The author introduces the most important facts about the country or region.

Globes A globe on which you can see the country's or region's position in the continent and the world.

Flags Every country's flag is shown.

Information panels Every country has an information panel, which gives its area, population, and capital and where possible its currency, religions, languages, major cities, and government.

Pictures Important features of each country are illustrated, with captions, to give a flavor of the country. You can find out about physical features, famous people, ordinary people, animals, plants, places, products, and much more.

Maps Every country is shown on a clear, accurate map. To get the most out of the maps it helps to know the symbols, which are shown in the key on the opposite page.

Land Coloring on the map shows where the land is forested, frozen, or desert.

Height Relief hill shading shows where the mountain ranges are. Individual mountains are marked by a triangle.

Direction Except for the map of the Arctic, all of the maps are drawn with north at the top of the page.

Scale All of the maps are drawn to scale so that you can find the distance between places in miles or kilometers.

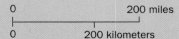

KEY TO MAPS

CONTENTS

FRANCE	Country name
Lapland	Region
⌒	Country border
■	More than 1 million people*
•	More than 500,000 people
·	Less than 500,000 people
☐	Country capital
ALPS	Mountain range
▲ *Mont Blanc 15,863 ft (4,807 m)*	Mountain with its height
∴ *Stonehenge*	Archaeological site

Rhine	River
	Canal
	Lake
─┼─	Dam
	Island

	Forest
	Crops
	Dry grassland
	Desert
	Tundra
	Polar

Many large cities, such as Birmingham, have metropolitan populations that are greater than the city figures. Such cities have larger dot sizes to emphasize their importance.

CONTINENT CLOSE-UPS

People and Beliefs Map of population densities; chart of percentage of population by country; chart of areas of countries; map of religions.

Climate and Vegetation Map of vegetation from polar to desert; maps of winter and summer temperatures; map of annual rainfall.

Ecology and Environment Map of environmental damage to land and sea; maps showing deaths caused by heart disease, cancers, and fatal road accidents; panel of endangered animals and plants.

Economy Map of agricultural and industrial products; chart of gross national product for individual countries; panel on per capita gross national products; map of sources of energy.

Politics and History Panel of great events; map of location of major events in European history; timeline of important dates; maps of prehistoric sites, the Roman Empire, 20th century-conflicts, and the European Community.

Oceans Maps of the Atlantic and Arctic oceans and panels of statistics.

Index All the names on the maps and in the picture captions can be found in the index at the end of the book.

Reindeer
see page 7

EUROPE

Europe is the sixth-largest continent, covering about seven percent of the world's land area. Only Australia is smaller. Europe was the home of several major civilizations, and its culture has had a great influence on the rest of the world.

In the east, Europe borders Asia. The boundary with Asia runs along the Ural Mountains and the Ural River to the Caspian Sea and then through the Caucasus Mountains. About one-quarter of Russia lies in Europe, while the rest is in Asia. Smaller parts of four other countries also lie in Europe.

European Union This is an alliance of 15 European countries that work together to create a single economy, promote democracy, and prevent wars. The headquarters is in Brussels (above), the parliament in Strasbourg.

Napoleon I (1769-1821) was a great military leader who became emperor of France. His armies conquered an empire that covered most of central and western Europe. Europe has been the scene of many great wars.

EUROPE
Area: 10,443,000 sq km (4,032,000 sq miles)
Population: 705,600,000
Number of independent countries: 43
(including European Russia but not Azerbaijan, Georgia, Kazakhstan, and Turkey, which are mainly in Asia)

ICELAND

ATLANTIC OCEAN

NORWAY

SWEDEN

North Sea

IRELAND

UNITED KINGDOM

DENMARK

Baltic Sea

NETHERLANDS

BELGIUM

GERMANY

POLAN

LUXEMBOURG

CZECH REP.

Bay of Biscay

FRANCE

LIECHTENSTEIN

SLOVA

SWITZERLAND

AUSTRIA

HUNGA

SLOVENIA

CROATIA

ANDORRA

MONACO

SAN MARINO

BOSNIA& HERZEGOVIN

PORTUGAL

SPAIN

ITALY

VATICAN CITY

GIBRALTAR (UK)

MEDITERRANEAN SEA

MALTA

0   250 miles
0   250 kilometers

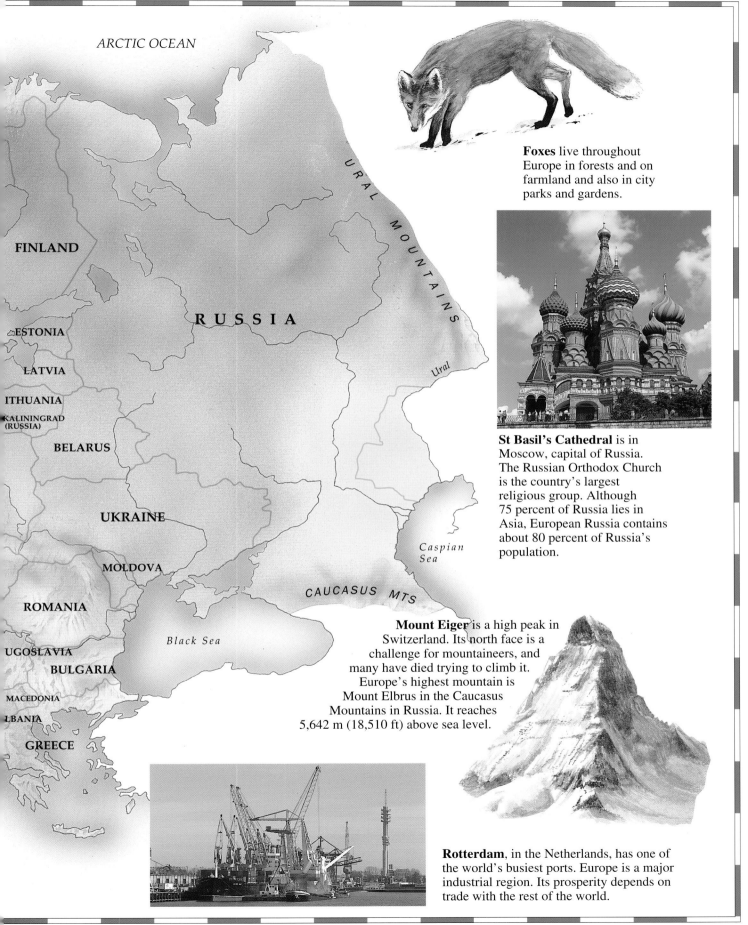

ARCTIC OCEAN

FINLAND

ESTONIA

LATVIA

ITHUANIA

KALININGRAD
(RUSSIA)

BELARUS

RUSSIA

UKRAINE

MOLDOVA

ROMANIA

UGOSLAVIA

BULGARIA

MACEDONIA

LBANIA

GREECE

URAL MOUNTAINS

Ural

Caspian
Sea

CAUCASUS MTS

Black Sea

Foxes live throughout
Europe in forests and on
farmland and also in city
parks and gardens.

St Basil's Cathedral is in
Moscow, capital of Russia.
The Russian Orthodox Church
is the country's largest
religious group. Although
75 percent of Russia lies in
Asia, European Russia contains
about 80 percent of Russia's
population.

Mount Eiger is a high peak in
Switzerland. Its north face is a
challenge for mountaineers, and
many have died trying to climb it.
Europe's highest mountain is
Mount Elbrus in the Caucasus
Mountains in Russia. It reaches
5,642 m (18,510 ft) above sea level.

Rotterdam, in the Netherlands, has one of
the world's busiest ports. Europe is a major
industrial region. Its prosperity depends on
trade with the rest of the world.

NORTHERN EUROPE

Northern Europe contains Scandinavia, a region that consists of Norway, Sweden, and the small country of Denmark. Finland is also sometimes considered a Scandinavian country.

   The climate is mostly unsuitable for farming, except in the south. The region's resources include Norway's oil, its many rivers, and huge forests. Manufacturing is now the most important economic activity in all four countries.

DENMARK

Area: 43,094 sq km (16,639 sq miles)
Highest point: 173 m (568 ft)
Population: 5,284,000
Capital and largest city: Copenhagen (pop 1,346,000, including suburbs)
Other large cities: Arhus (209,000)
Odense (143,000)
Alborg (117,000)
Official language: Danish
Religions: Christianity (Lutheran 87%)
Government: Monarchy
Currency: Danish krone

FINLAND

Area: 338,145 sq km (130,559 sq miles)
Highest point: Mount Haltia 1,324 m (4,344 ft)
Population: 5,140,000
Capital and largest city: Helsinki (pop 875,000, including suburbs)
Other large cities: Tampere (186,000)
Turku (167,000)
Oulu (112,000)
Official languages: Finnish, Swedish
Religions: Christianity (Lutheran 86%)
Government: Republic
Currency: Markka, Euro

NORWAY

Area: 323,877 sq km (125,050 sq miles)
Highest point: Galdhøppigen 2469 m (8,100 ft)
Population: 4,404,000
Capital and largest city: Oslo (pop 494,000)
Other large cities: Bergen (224,000)
Trondheim (145,000)
Stavanger (108,000)
Official language: Norwegian
Religions: Christianity (Lutheran 88%)
Government: Monarchy
Currency: Norwegian krone

Fjords are long, narrow inlets of sea that stretch along the ragged, mountainous coast of Norway. One of them, called Sogne Fjord, extends 200 km (124 miles) inland.

Oil is extracted from deposits under the North Sea. Fuels and fuel products are Norway's leading exports. Farming, forestry, fishing, and manufacturing are major economic activities in northern Europe.

SWEDEN

Area: 449,964 sq km (173,732 sq miles)
Highest point: Mount Kebnekaise 2,111 m (6,926 ft)
Population: 8,849,000
Capital and largest city: Stockholm (pop 718,000)
Other large cities: Göteborg (454,000)
Malmö (248,000)
Official language: Swedish
Religions: Christianity (Church of Sweden 86%)
Government: Monarchy
Currency: Swedish krona

ATLANTIC
OCEAN

Trondheim

Ålesund

Galdhøppigen
8,100 ft
(2,469 m)

Bergen

NORWAY

Glåma

Oslo

Stavanger

Skien

Fredrikstad

Kristiansand

Lake
Vänern

Skagerrak

Lake
Vättern

Borås

Göteborg

North
Sea

Ålborg

Kattegat

Växjö

Jutland

568 ft Århus
(173 m)

DENMARK

Esbjerg

Copenhagen

Odense

Malmö

Bornholm

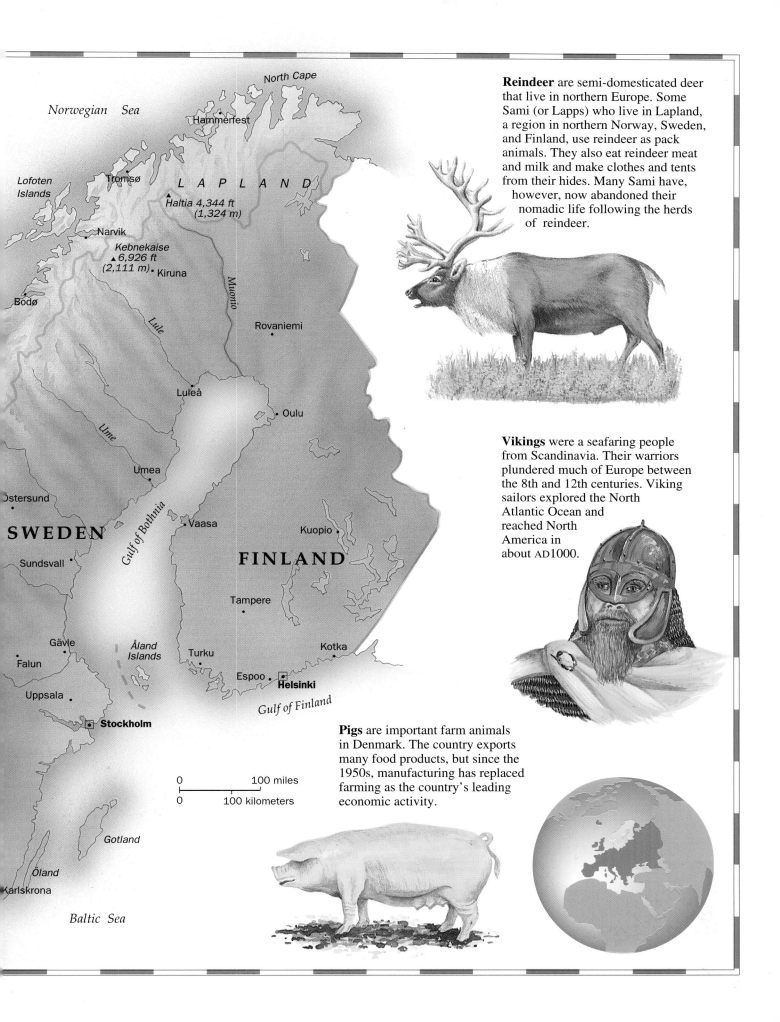

Norwegian Sea

North Cape

Hammerfest

Lofoten
Islands

L A P L A N D

Tromsø

Haltia 4,344 ft
(1,324 m)

Narvik

Kebnekaise
▲ 6,926 ft
(2,111 m) • Kiruna

Muonio

Bodø

Lule

Rovaniemi

Luleå

• Oulu

Ume

Umea

Östersund

SWEDEN

Gulf of Bothnia

• Vaasa

Kuopio •

FINLAND

Sundsvall •

Tampere

Gävle

Åland
Islands

Falun

Turku

Kotka

Uppsala

Espoo • □ Helsinki

Gulf of Finland

□ Stockholm

Gotland

Öland

Karlskrona

Baltic Sea

0   100 miles

0   100 kilometers

Reindeer are semi-domesticated deer that live in northern Europe. Some Sami (or Lapps) who live in Lapland, a region in northern Norway, Sweden, and Finland, use reindeer as pack animals. They also eat reindeer meat and milk and make clothes and tents from their hides. Many Sami have, however, now abandoned their nomadic life following the herds of reindeer.

Vikings were a seafaring people from Scandinavia. Their warriors plundered much of Europe between the 8th and 12th centuries. Viking sailors explored the North Atlantic Ocean and reached North America in about AD1000.

Pigs are important farm animals in Denmark. The country exports many food products, but since the 1950s, manufacturing has replaced farming as the country's leading economic activity.

ICELAND

Iceland, in the North Atlantic Ocean, is often called the "land of ice and fire." Large bodies of ice cover about one-eighth of the land, and the country has about 200 volcanoes. The main industry is fishing and fish processing.

ICELAND

Area: 103,000 sq km (39,769 sq miles)
Highest point: Hvannadalshnúkur 2,119 m (6,952 ft)
Population: 271,000
Capital: Reykjavik (pop 105,000)
Official language: Icelandic
Religions: Christianity (Lutheran 90%)
Government: Republic
Currency: Icelandic krona

Geysers are hot springs that throw up high jets of steam and hot water. The water is heated by underground volcanic rocks. It is used to heat buildings and supply homes with hot tap water.

Fishing is important in the waters around Iceland. Fish and fish products account for more than seven-tenths of the country's exports. Iceland has little farmland, though some farmers raise sheep and cattle.

Isafjördhur

Siglufjördhur

Blönduos · · Akureyri

Seydisfjördhur

I C E L A N D

Hofn

V a t n a j ö k u l l

Reykjavik
Hafnarfjördhur

▲ Hvannadalshnúkur
6,952 ft (2,119 m)

ATLANTIC OCEAN

Heimaey

Vik

Surtsey

| 0 | | 50 miles |
| 0 | | 50 kilometers |

Surtsey is a volcanic island that appeared off southern Iceland in 1963. It was named after Surt, the Norse god of fire.

IRELAND

Ireland consists of the Republic of Ireland, which
makes up five-sixths of the island, and Northern Ireland,
which is part of the United Kingdom (see page 10).
Farming is important in Ireland, but manufacturing
and new technology and service industries are the most
important economic activities.

Giant's Causeway is probably
Northern Ireland's best-known
tourist attraction. It was formed
when molten lava cooled to
form masses of six-sided
columns made of a rock
called basalt.

IRELAND

Area: 70,284 sq km (27,137 sq miles)
Highest point:
Carrauntoohill 1,041 m (3,141 ft)
Population: 3,661,000
Capital and largest city: Dublin (pop 481,000)
Other large cities: Cork (127,000)
Official languages: Irish, English
Religions: Christianity (Roman Catholic 92%)
Government: Republic
Currency: Irish pound, Euro

Shamrock is Ireland's
national symbol. It is a
kind of clover that,
according to legend,
St Patrick planted. Its
three leaves represent
the Holy Trinity.

Giant's Causeway

Coleraine

Londonderry

Bann

Antrim

**NORTHERN
IRELAND**

Omagh

*Lough
Neagh*

Belfast

Lurgan

*Lower
Lough Erne*

Portadown

*Upper Lough
Erne*

Newry

Sligo

Dundalk

*Lough
Conn*

Carrick-on-Shannon

*Lough
Mask*

I R E L A N D

Drogheda

IRISH SEA

*Lough
Ree*

*Lough
Corrib*

Athlone

Galway

Shannon

Liffey

Dublin

Galway Bay

Roscrea

*Lough
Derg*

Wicklow

Barrow

*ATLANTIC
OCEAN*

Limerick

Clonmel

Waterford

Wexford

Tralee

Killarney

Carrauntoohill
3,141 ft (1,041 m)

Lee

Cork

0   50 miles
0   50 kilometers

Celtic crosses and other
carved stone monuments
are found throughout
Ireland.

Potatoes, barley, sugar beets,
and wheat are leading crops
in Ireland. Cattle, pigs, and
sheep are important farm
animals.

9

UNITED KINGDOM

The United Kingdom of Great Britain and Northern Ireland (often called the UK, or Britain) includes England, Scotland, and Wales, which are together called Great Britain, and Northern Ireland (see map on page 9).

(see map on page 9)

The Industrial Revolution began in England in the late 18th century, and today the country plays a major part in world trade. It is the most densely populated country in Europe.

UNITED KINGDOM

Area: 243,305 sq km (93,941 sq miles)
Highest point: Ben Nevis 1,343 m (4,406 ft)
Population: 59,200,000
Capital and largest city: London (pop 7,074,000)
Other large cities: Birmingham (1,020,000)
Leeds (727,000)
Official language: English
Religions: Christianity (66%)
Government: Monarchy
Currency: Pound sterling

ENGLAND
Area: 130,395 sq km (50,346 sq miles)
Population: 49,500,000
Capital: London (pop 7,074,000)

NORTHERN IRELAND
Area: 13,843 sq km (5,345 sq miles)
Population: 1,700,000
Capital: Belfast (pop 284,000)

SCOTLAND
Area: 78,313 sq km (30,237 sq miles)
Population: 5,100,000
Capital: Edinburgh (pop 450,000)

WALES
Area: 20,754 sq km (8,013 sq miles)
Population: 2,900,000
Capital: Cardiff (pop 321,000)

ISLE OF MAN & CHANNEL ISLANDS
The Isle of Man in the Irish Sea and the Channel Islands off the coast of northwest France are British dependencies, but they are not part of the United Kingdom.

William Shakespeare (1564-1616) is widely regarded as the world's greatest poet and dramatist. Britain has also produced many other celebrated writers, and English is now spoken in many countries.

Stonehenge is an ancient monument in southern England. It is a circle of huge stones, that were probably used for religious purposes. It was built between about 2800 and 1500 BC.

Sheep are raised in highland areas, cattle and pigs on lowland farms. Agriculture is important, but the UK imports food. Most of its wealth comes from manufacturing, trade, and services such as banking, insurance, finance, and tourism.

John o' Groats
Wick
Lewis
North West Highlands
Hebrides
Skye
Inverness
Loch Ness
Spey
Fort William
Ben Nevis 4,406 ft (1,343 m)
Grampian Mt
Dundee
Perth
Loch Lomond
SCOTLAND
Glasgow
Clyde
Edinburgh
Ayr
Dumfries
Carlis
Isle of Man
Scafell Pike 3,227 ft (978
Douglas
Blackpool
Liverpool
Bangor
Snowdon 3,580 ft (1,085 m)
IRISH SEA
WALES
Aberystwyth
Swansea
Newp
Cardiff
Bristo
Exeter
Plymouth
Penzance
Land's End
Isles of Scilly

Orkney Islands

•Wick

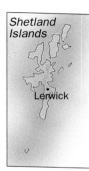

Shetland Islands

Lerwick

Aberdeen

Golf developed in Scotland, where the first organized golf club was set up in 1744. Soccer is, however, by far the most popular sport in the United Kingdom.

NORTH SEA

Berwick-upon-Tweed

Newcastle upon Tyne
•Sunderland

•Middlesbrough

•York
•Bradford
Leeds
Kingston upon Hull

Manchester
•Sheffield

oke-on-Trent
Derby• •Nottingham

ENGLAND
•Leicester   Norwich•

Wolverhampton
■ •Coventry
Birmingham   Cambridge•
Northampton
•Ipswich

Oxford   •Luton
Thames ■**London**
Reading
Stonehenge   Dover•

Southampton Brighton
Bournemouth Portsmouth
•
Isle of Wight

English Channel

London Eye Built by the River Thames to mark the millennium, this is the largest observation wheel in the world. From the top you can see for 25 miles (40 km).

Puffins are sea birds found mostly on the north and west coasts of Britain. The country has many animal species, though numbers have declined because of human population pressures and pollution.

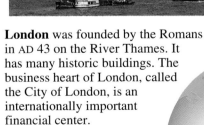

London was founded by the Romans in AD 43 on the River Thames. It has many historic buildings. The business heart of London, called the City of London, is an internationally important financial center.

Channel Islands

Guernsey
FRANCE

Jersey

0   50 miles
0   50 kilometers

Low Countries

The Low Countries lie at the western end of a huge plain that extends across Europe from the North Sea to the Ural Mountains in Russia. Much of the land is flat. Large areas, especially in the Netherlands, were once under the sea. They would still be flooded if the Dutch had not built dikes (strong sea walls). Farming is important in this region, but manufacturing is the most important economic activity.

BELGIUM

Area: 30,519 sq km (11,783 sq miles)
Highest point:
Botrange Mountain 694 m (2,277 ft)
Population: 10,190,000
Capital and largest city: Brussels (pop 948,000)
Other large cities: Antwerp (456,000)
Ghent (226,000)
Official languages: Flemish, French, German
Religions: Christianity (Roman Catholic 88%)
Government: Federal monarchy
Currency: Belgian franc, Euro

LUXEMBOURG

Area: 2,586 sq km (998 sq miles)
Highest point: Buurgplatz 559 m (1,835 ft)
Population: 422,000
Capital: Luxembourg (pop 76,000)
Languages: Luxemburgian, French, German
Religions: Christianity (Roman Catholic 95%)
Government: Monarchy (Grand Duchy)
Currency: Luxembourg franc, Euro

NETHERLANDS

Area: 40,844 sq km (15,770 sq miles)
Highest point: 321 m (1,053 ft)
Population: 15,607,000
Capital and largest city: Amsterdam
(pop 718,000)
Other large cities: Rotterdam (593,000)
The Hague (442,000)
Official language: Dutch
Religions: Christianity (Roman Catholic 32%,
Dutch Reform Church 15%, Calvinist 8%)
Government: Monarchy
Currency: Guilder, Euro

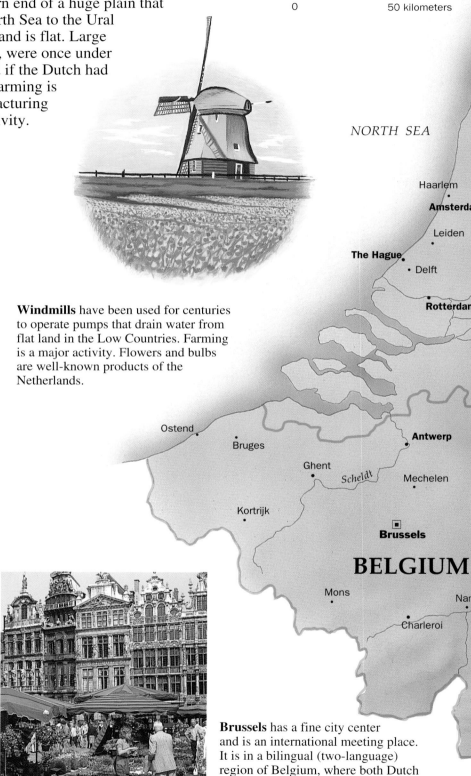

Windmills have been used for centuries to operate pumps that drain water from flat land in the Low Countries. Farming is a major activity. Flowers and bulbs are well-known products of the Netherlands.

Brussels has a fine city center and is an international meeting place. It is in a bilingual (two-language) region of Belgium, where both Dutch and French are spoken. Other regions include the Flemish region in the north and the French-speaking Walloon region in the south.

NETHERLANDS

Frisian Islands

Leeuwarden

Groningen

Barrier Dam

IJsselmeer

Zwolle

IJssel

Apeldoorn

Almelo

Enschede

Utrecht

Rhine

Arnhem

Nijmegen

's-Hertogenbosch

Tilburg

Maas

Eindhoven

Genk

Heerlen

1,053 ft (321 m)

Maastricht

Liège

Botrange ▲
2,227 ft
(694 m)

Ardennes

Buurgplatz 1,835 ft
(559 m)

LUXEMBOURG

Luxembourg

Esch-sur-Alzette

Barges are used to transport goods along rivers and canals. Rotterdam in the Netherlands and Antwerp in Belgium are among the world's busiest ports.

Computers and electronic products are important in the Netherlands. The country also produces many other technically advanced goods. Belgium is famous for its ancient textile industry, while Luxembourg is a major steel producer.

Bicycles and motorcycles are popular means of transportation in the Low countries. The Low Countries have a good network of paved roads, and most families own a car.

Grand Ducal Palace This is the home of the Grand Duke (or Duchess) of Luxembourg, the country's head of state. Though the countries are all democracies, the Low Countries have a long monarchist tradition.

GERMANY

In 1945, at the end of World War II, Germany was in ruins. From 1949, it was divided into two parts. West Germany, with aid from western countries including the United States, recovered quickly from the war. It soon became a prosperous industrial democracy. East Germany, under a Communist government, was much less prosperous. The two Germanies were reunited in 1990. This was the first of several major changes to the map of Europe that occurred during the 1990s.

GERMANY

Area: 356,980 sq km (137,831 sq miles)
Highest point: Zugspitze, near the Austrian border, 2,963 m (9,721 ft)
Population: 82,071,000
Capital and largest city: Berlin (pop 3,470,000)
Other large cities: Hamburg (1,707,000)
Munich (1,240,000)
Cologne (964,000)
Frankfurt-am-Main (651,000)
Essen (616,000)
Official language: German
Religions: Christianity (Lutheran 41%, Roman Catholic 34%), Islam 2%
Government: Federal republic
Currency: Mark, Euro

Storks can often be seen perching on nests on chimney pots. Birds and other wildlife in Germany have suffered from pollution, including acid rain, which has damaged the country's forests.

Printing The invention of movable type in the mid-15th century by the German Johannes Gutenberg made book production and education easier. The Gutenberg Bible was the first Bible produced by movable type.

Brandenburg Gate This monument, built in Berlin in 1791, later became a symbol of a divided Europe. It stood close to the wall that the communist East German government built to prevent unauthorized crossings to the West.

NORTH SEA

Flensbu

Bremerhaven

Hambur

Oldenburg

Bremen

Osnabrück

Hanove

Münster

Bielefeld

Weser

Dortmund

Duisburg

Essen

Düsseldorf

Wuppertal

Mönchengladbach

Kassel

Aachen

Cologne

G E R M

Bonn

Rhine

Koblenz

Eifel

Mosel

Frankfurt-am-Main

Wiesbaden

Mainz

Darmstadt

Mannheim

Saarbrücken

Karlsruhe

Bâden-Baden

Stuttgart

Black Forest

Ulm

Freiburg

Ravensburg

Lake Constance

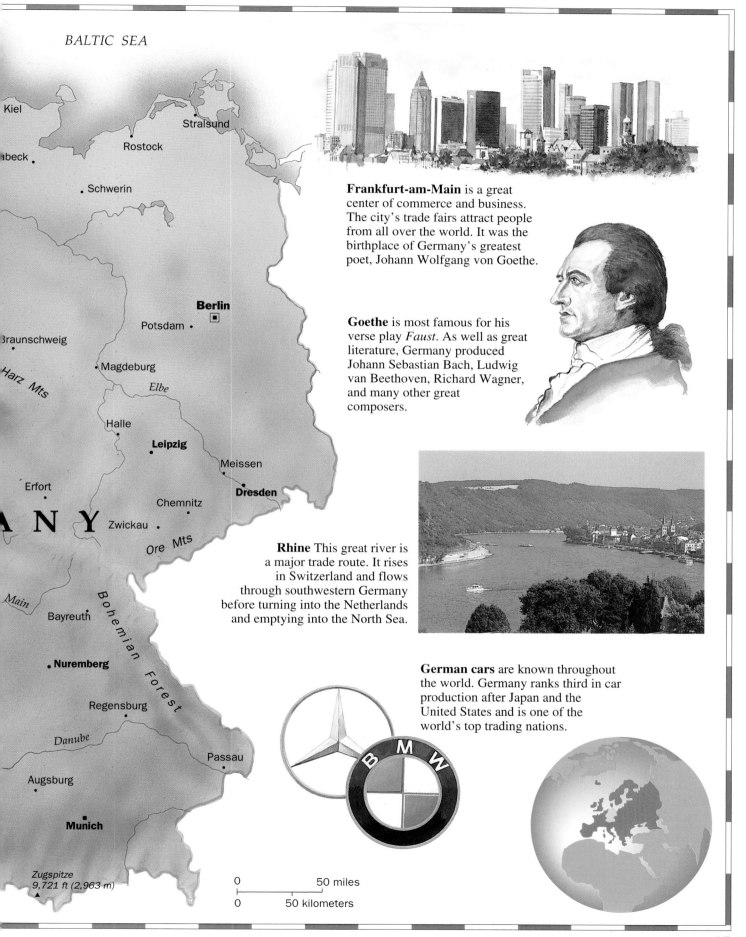

Kiel

Stralsund

Rostock

ıbeck

Schwerin

Berlin
■

Potsdam

Braunschweig

Magdeburg

Elbe

Harz Mts

Halle

Leipzig

Meissen

Erfort

Dresden

Chemnitz

ıNY

Zwickau

Ore Mts

Main

Bohemian Forest

Bayreuth

Nuremberg

Regensburg

Danube

Passau

Augsburg

Munich

Zugspitze
9,721 ft (2,963 m)
▲

0   50 miles

0   50 kilometers

Frankfurt-am-Main is a great center of commerce and business. The city's trade fairs attract people from all over the world. It was the birthplace of Germany's greatest poet, Johann Wolfgang von Goethe.

Goethe is most famous for his verse play *Faust*. As well as great literature, Germany produced Johann Sebastian Bach, Ludwig van Beethoven, Richard Wagner, and many other great composers.

Rhine This great river is a major trade route. It rises in Switzerland and flows through southwestern Germany before turning into the Netherlands and emptying into the North Sea.

German cars are known throughout the world. Germany ranks third in car production after Japan and the United States and is one of the world's top trading nations.

15

MIDDLE EUROPE

Middle Europe consists of Switzerland, Austria, and the tiny principality of Liechtenstein, which is sandwiched between them. Western Europe's highest mountain range, the Alps, runs through the region. The magnificent scenery and winter sports draw many tourists to the area. Manufacturing is important, and the countries are prosperous. Switzerland is famous for its banks, which attract investors from all over the world.

AUSTRIA

Area: 83,859sq km (32,378 sq miles)
Highest point: Gross Glockner 3,797m (12,547 ft)
Population: 8,072,000
Capital and largest city: Vienna (pop,1,540,000)
Other large cities: Graz (238,000)
Official language: German
Religions: Christianity (Roman Catholic 75%)
Government: Federal republic
Currency: Schilling, Euro

SWITZERLAND

Area: 41,284 sq km (15,940 sq miles)
Highest point: Dufourspitze of Monte Rosa 4,634m (15,203 ft)
Population: 7,088,000
Capital: Bern (pop 134,000)
Largest cities: Zurich (344,000)
Basel (174,000)
Official languages: French, German, Italian
Religions: Christianity (Roman Catholic 46%, Protestant 40%)
Government: Federal republic
Currency: Swiss franc

LIECHTENSTEIN

Area: 160sq km (62 sq miles)
Population: 31,000
Capital: Vaduz (pop 5,000)
Official language: German
Religions: Christianity (Roman Catholic 80%)
Government: Monarchy (principality)
Currency: Swiss franc

Watches and precision instruments are famous Swiss products. Switzerland lacks natural resources. Its skilled workers use imported materials to make valuable products.

Alps This magnificent, snow-capped range extends from France, through Switzerland, Austria, and northern Italy, into Slovenia. The highest peak in the Alps is Mont Blanc in France (see pages 18-19).

Postage stamps provide a useful source of income for Liechtenstein. Many stamps prized by collectors show paintings that belong to the country's prince.

Lake Constance
Basel   *Rhine*   Winterthur   Konstanz
Aaråu   Zurich   Sankt Gallen   .Dornbirn
Zurichsee
Neuchâtel   Bern   Lucerne   Vaduz
Lake Neuchâtel   LIECHTENSTEIN
SWITZERLAND   *Rhine*   .Chur   L
Lausanne   A
Lake Geneva
Geneva   *Rhône*   Locarno   Lugano
Matterhorn 14,777 ft (4,478 m)   *Lake Maggiore*
Monte Rosa 15,203 ft (4,634 m)

0   100 miles
0   100 kilometers

Pharmaceuticals (chemicals used in medicine) are made in both Austria and Switzerland. Austria produces many luxury goods, such as fine glassware and jewelry, but metals and metal goods are the chief products and exports.

Wolfgang Amadeus Mozart (1756-91) was born in Salzburg, Austria, and started to compose and perform as a child. He is considered one of the greatest of all musical geniuses. Other great Austrian composers include Joseph Haydn, Franz Schubert and Gustav Mahler.

Edelweiss is a plant with white, star-shaped flowers that grows in the Alps. The upper parts of the Alps are treeless, and the vegetation resembles that of the tundra in the Arctic regions of northern Europe.

Krems

Vienna

Linz

Danube

Sankt Pölten

Lake Neusiedler

Wels

Steyr

Enns

Wiener Neustadt

Salzburg

A U S T R I A

Leoben

Inn

Salzach

Graz

Mur

Innsbruck

S

Gross Glockner
12,547 ft
(3,797m)

P

Villach

Klagenfurt

Skiing is a popular winter sport in the Alps. St. Moritz and Zermatt are major resorts in Switzerland, while St Anton has some of the world's most challenging ski slopes. Austrian resorts include Innsbruck and Salzburg.

FRANCE

France is the largest country in western Europe. It has a beautiful landscape and fine cities with many historic buildings. It is also one of the world's top manufacturing nations, and Paris is a world center of the fashion industry. Agriculture employs only seven percent of the population, but France is western Europe's leading producer of farm products. France is famous for its excellent food and wines and is one of the most prosperous countries in Europe.

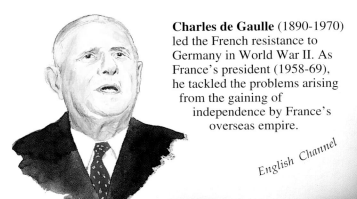

Charles de Gaulle (1890-1970) led the French resistance to Germany in World War II. As France's president (1958-69), he tackled the problems arising from the gaining of independence by France's overseas empire.

FRANCE

Area: 551,500 sq km (212,935 sq miles)
Highest point: Mont Blanc 4,807 m (15,771 ft)
Population: 58,607,000
Capital and largest city: Paris (pop 9,060,000 including suburbs)
Other large cities: Lyon (1,262,000)
Marseille (1,231,000)
Bordeaux (685,000)
Toulouse (608,000)
Nantes (492,000)
Nice (457,000)
Strasbourg (338,000)
Official language: French
Religions: Christianity (Roman Catholic 76%), Islam 5.5%
Government: Republic
Currency: French franc, Euro

MONACO

Area: 1.5 sq km (0.6 sq miles)
Population: 32,000
Capital: Monaco
Official language: French
Religions: Christianity (officially Roman Catholic)
Government: Monarchy under French protection
Currency: French franc

Eiffel Tower This wrought-iron tower in Paris is the city's most famous landmark. It was built for the World Fair of 1889. Paris is a great center of the arts and education and also a major industrial city.

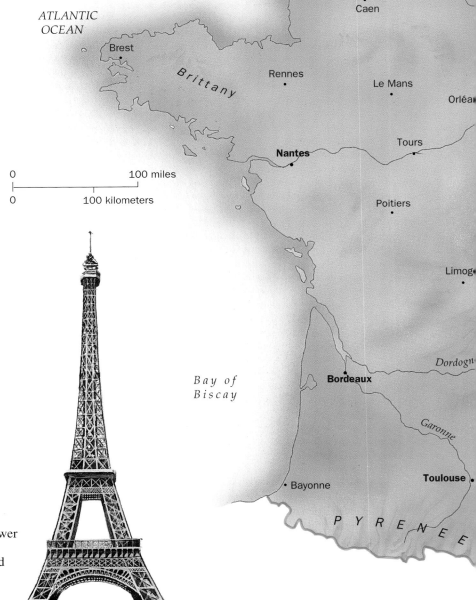

ATLANTIC OCEAN

Cala

English Channel

Cherbourg

Le Havre

Rouen

Caen

Brest

Brittany

Rennes

Le Mans

Orléa

Nantes

Tours

Poitiers

0   100 miles
0   100 kilometers

Limog

Bay of Biscay

Bordeaux

Dordogn

Garonne

Bayonne

Toulouse

P Y R E N E E

Good food and top-quality wines are features of everyday life in France. French cooking is copied around the world. Nearly every region has its own special recipes.

High-speed trains link Paris to other cities in France. The railway system, which is owned and operated by the government, provides excellent passenger and goods services.

Painting France has produced many great painters and influential artistic movements such as Impressionism. Magnificent architecture, including superb churches, fine literature, and music are other art forms at which the French excel.

Car rallies are among Monaco's many tourist attractions. The principality, on the southeast coast of France, is one of the world's tiniest independent countries. Important events include the Monaco Grand Prix and the Monte Carlo Rally.

Lille

Lens

Amiens

Reims

Metz

Strasbourg

■ **Paris**

Nancy

Meuse

Rhine

Seine

Troyes

Loire

Dijon

Besançon

Saône

FRANCE

Lake Geneva

Clermont Ferrand

Lyon

Mt Blanc 15,771 ft (4,807m)

Massif Central

Saint Étienne

Grenoble

Rhône

A L P S

Avignon

MONACO

Nice

Monte Carlo

Cannes

Montpellier

Marseille

Toulon

Perpignan

MEDITERRANEAN SEA

Bastia

Corsica

Ajaccio

IBERIAN PENINSULA

The Iberian Peninsula consists of two large countries, Spain and Portugal, together with the tiny state of Andorra, in the Pyrenees Mountains in the northeast, and Gibraltar, a small British territory, in the far south. The Canary Islands off the coast of Africa also belong to Spain.

Spain is western Europe's second-largest country after France. Spain's economy was shattered by a civil war (1936-39), but since the 1950s it has developed into a fairly prosperous nation. Portugal was a dictatorship from 1933 until 1968. Since 1968, its economy has grown, but it remains one of the poorer members of the European Union.

SPAIN

Area: 505,992 sq km (195,365 sq miles)
Highest point: Pico de Teide, in the Canary Islands, 3,718 m (12,198 ft)
Population: 39,323,000
Capital and largest city: Madrid (pop 2,867,000)
Other large cities: Barcelona (1,509,000) Valencia (747,000)
Languages: Castilian Spanish (official), Basque, Catalan, Galician
Religions: Christianity (Roman Catholic 67%)
Government: Monarchy
Currency: Peseta, Euro

PORTUGAL

Area: 91,982 sq km (35,514 sq miles)
Highest point: Estrela,1,993 m (6,539 ft)
Population: 9,945,000
Capital and largest city: Lisbon (pop 663,000)
Other large cities: Oporto (302,000)
Official language: Portuguese
Religions: Christianity (Roman Catholic 92%)
Government: Republic
Currency: Escudo, Euro

ANDORRA

Area: 453 sq km (175 sq miles)
Highest point: Coma Pedrosa 2,946 m (9,665 ft)
Population: 64,000
Capital: Andorra La Vella (pop 17,000)
Official language: Catalan
Religions: Christianity (Roman Catholic 92%)
Government: Principality
Currency: French franc, Spanish peseta

Bay of Biscay

Gijón
Santan

La Coruña

Oviedo

Santiago de Compostela

Cantabrian Mts

Vigo

León

Orense

Bur

ATLANTIC OCEAN

Braga

Valladolid

Duero

Oporto *Douro*

Salamanca

Estrela
6,539 ft (1,993 m)

Coimbra

Mad

PORTUGAL

Tajo (Tagus)

To

Cáceres   **S P A I N**

Guadiana

Lisbon

Setúbal

Badajoz

Evora

Linar

Guadalqu

Córdoba

Huelva   **Seville**

Lagos

Grana
Sierr

Faro

Jerez de la Frontera   **Málaga**

Cadiz

Gibraltar (UK)

| 0 | 100 miles |
| 0 | 100 kilometers |

Canary Islands (Spain)

ATLANTIC OCEAN

La Palma

Lanzarote

Tenerife   Santa Cruz

Gomera

Las Palmas   Fuerteventura

Pico de Teide
12198 ft
(3,718 m)

Hierro

Gran Canaria

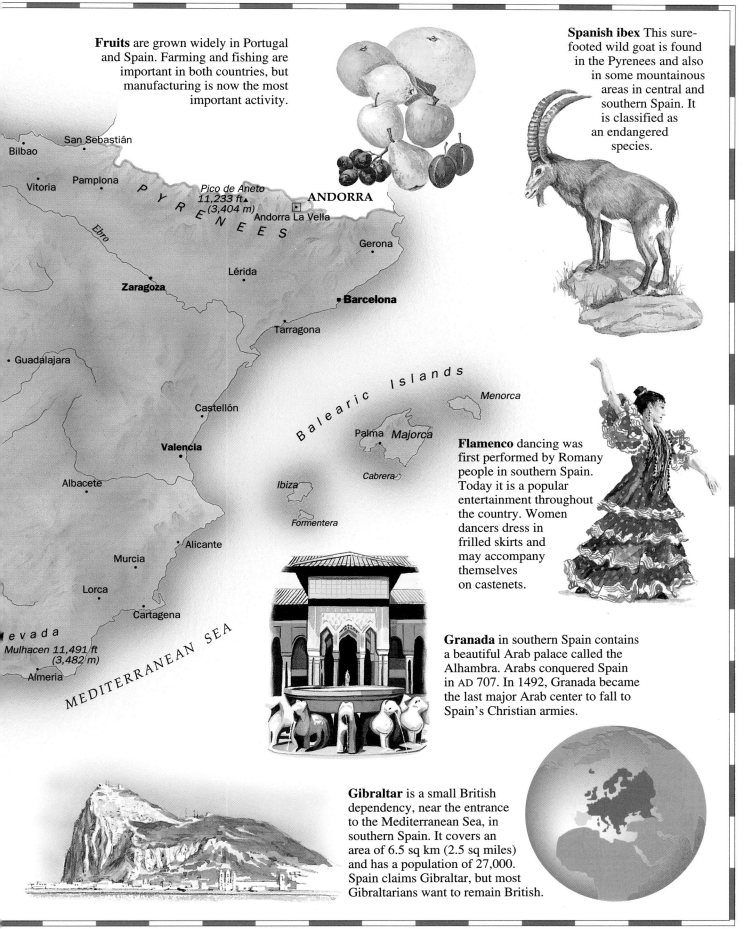

Fruits are grown widely in Portugal and Spain. Farming and fishing are important in both countries, but manufacturing is now the most important activity.

Spanish ibex This sure-footed wild goat is found in the Pyrenees and also in some mountainous areas in central and southern Spain. It is classified as an endangered species.

Bilbao

San Sebastián

Vitoria

Pamplona

P Y R E N E E S

Ebro

Pico de Aneto
11,233 ft▲
(3,404 m)

ANDORRA

Andorra La Vella

Gerona

Lérida

Zaragoza

■ **Barcelona**

Tarragona

• Guadalajara

Balearic Islands

Castellón

Menorca

Palma *Majorca*

Valencia

Cabrera

Albacete

Ibiza

Formentera

Murcia

• Alicante

Lorca

Cartagena

e v a d a

Mulhacen 11,491 ft
(3,482 m)

Almería

MEDITERRANEAN SEA

Flamenco dancing was first performed by Romany people in southern Spain. Today it is a popular entertainment throughout the country. Women dancers dress in frilled skirts and may accompany themselves on castenets.

Granada in southern Spain contains a beautiful Arab palace called the Alhambra. Arabs conquered Spain in AD 707. In 1492, Granada became the last major Arab center to fall to Spain's Christian armies.

Gibraltar is a small British dependency, near the entrance to the Mediterranean Sea, in southern Spain. It covers an area of 6.5 sq km (2.5 sq miles) and has a population of 27,000. Spain claims Gibraltar, but most Gibraltarians want to remain British.

ITALY

Italy extends like a leg and foot into the Mediterranean Sea. The Alps in the far north overlook the fertile Po River basin, where most of Italy's major industrial cities are situated. The "leg" of Italy contains the Apennine Mountains. In the southwest are some active volcanoes, including Etna on the island of Sicily.

Two tiny independent nations lie inside Italy. They are San Marino and Vatican City, which covers an area about the size of a town park in the city of Rome. South of Sicily is the island nation of Malta.

ITALY

Area: 301,268 sq km (116,320 sq miles)
Highest point: Mont Blanc 4,807 m (15,771 ft)
Population: 57,523,000
Capital and largest city: Rome (pop 2,654,000)
Other large cities: Milan (1,306,000)
Naples (1,050,000)
Turin (923,000)
Official language: Italian
Religions: Christianity (Roman Catholic 82%)
Government: Republic
Currency: Lira, Euro

MALTA

Area: 316 sq km (122 sq miles)
Population: 375,000
Capital: Valletta (pop 9,000)
Official languages: Maltese, English
Religions: Christianity (Roman Catholic 93%)
Government: Republic
Currency: Maltese lira

SAN MARINO

Area: 61 sq km (24 sq miles)
Population: 26,000
Capital: San Marino (pop,5,000)
Official language: Italian
Religions: Christianity (Roman Catholic 89%)
Government: Republic
Currency: Italian lira

VATICAN CITY

Area: 0.44sq km (0.17 sq miles)
Population: 1,000
Government: Papacy
Currency: Italian lira

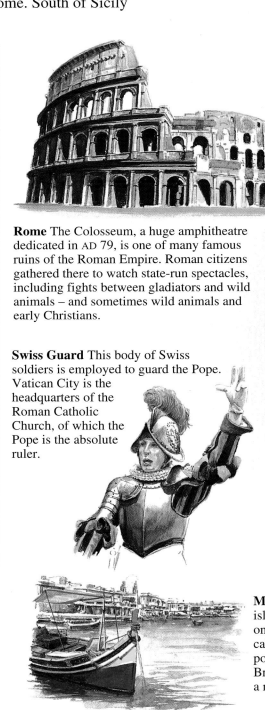

Rome The Colosseum, a huge amphitheatre dedicated in AD 79, is one of many famous ruins of the Roman Empire. Roman citizens gathered there to watch state-run spectacles, including fights between gladiators and wild animals – and sometimes wild animals and early Christians.

Swiss Guard This body of Swiss soldiers is employed to guard the Pope. Vatican City is the headquarters of the Roman Catholic Church, of which the Pope is the absolute ruler.

Malta consists of several islands south of Sicily. Valletta, on the largest island, which is also called Malta, is the capital and chief port. Malta became independent from Britain in 1964, though Britain kept a naval base there until 1979.

Mt Blanc 15,771 ft (4,807 m)
Lake Maggiore
Lake Como
Como
Bergamo
Milan
Turin
Genoa
Parma
La Spezia
San Remo
Pisa
Livorno
Elba
Sassari
Sardinia
Cagliari
MEDITERRANEAN

Venice is a city built on about 120 islands in the Adriatic Sea. Its streets are canals lined with beautiful buildings that are increasingly threatened by flooding, pollution, and overcrowding by tourists. Italy's cities, historic sites, and beautiful beaches attract more than 50 million tourists to the country each year.

Style Elegant fashions and stylish cars are products that have given Italy its worldwide reputation for excellence in design. Around 50 years ago, Italy was mainly a farming country, but it has grown increasingly rich through manufacturing.

Garibaldi (1807-82) Giuseppe Garibaldi was a military hero who fought to unite Italy. In 1860, with the help of 1,000 volunteers known as *red shirts*, he conquered Sicily and Naples.

Pompeii is an ancient Roman town near Naples. In AD 79 it was buried by volcanic ash that erupted from nearby Mount Vesuvius. The volcano has erupted many times since, the last time in 1944.

Bolzano
Trento
Udine
Treviso
Verona
Adige
Venice
Trieste
Padova
Modena
Bologna
Ravenna
Rimini
San Marino
SAN MARINO
Florence
Arno
Ancona
Perugia
Assisi
Tiber
Pescara
Rome
VATICAN CITY
Foggia
ITALY
Adriatic Sea
Bari
Naples
Vesuvius
Pompeii
Salerno
Potenza
Brindisi
Taranto
Tyrrhenian Sea
Catanzaro
Ustica
Lipari Is
Palermo
Messina
Trapani
Reggio di Calabria
Etna
11,022 ft (3,340 m)
Catania
Sicily
Licata
SEA
Pantelleria
MALTA
Valletta

0   100 miles
0   100 kilometers

GREECE AND THE BALKANS

This region in southeastern Europe includes Greece, the center of a great ancient civilization, Albania, and five countries which, until the early 1990s, made up the Communist country of Yugoslavia. Following the breakup of Yugoslavia, civil wars in Bosnia and Herzegovina, Croatia, and in the Kosovo region of the new Yugoslavia caused great damage and loss of life. The region's land is mostly rugged. Farming is important, but manufacturing is the most important economic activity.

GREECE

Area: 131,957 sq km (50,949 sq miles)
Population: 10,522,000
Capital: Athens (pop 3,073,000 including suburbs)
Official language: Greek
Religions: Christianity (Eastern Orthodox 94%)
Government: Republic
Currency: Drachma

SLOVENIA

Area: 20,256 sq km (7,821 sq miles)
Population: 1,986,000
Capital: Ljubljana (pop 270,000)
Official language: Slovene
Religions: Christianity (Roman Catholic 83%)
Government: Republic
Currency: Tolar

CROATIA

Area: 88,117 sq km (34,022 sq miles)
Population: 4,768,000
Capital: Zagreb (pop 868,000)
Official language: Croatian (Serbo-Croatian)
Religions: Christianity (Roman Catholic 72%, Eastern Orthodox 14%)
Government: Republic
Currency: Kuna

BOSNIA AND HERZEGOVINA

Area: 51,129 sq km (19,741 sq miles)
Population: 2,346,000
Capital: Sarajevo (pop 360,000)
Official language: Bosnian (Serbo-Croatian)
Religions: Christianity 42%, Islam 40%
Currency: Marka

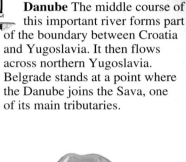

Area: 28,748 sq km (11,100 sq miles)
Population: 3,324,000
Capital: Tirana (pop 243,000)
Official language: Albanian
Religions: Islam 70%, Christianity 17%
Government: Republic
Currency: Lek

MACEDONIA

Area: 25,713 sq km (9,928 sq miles)
Population: 1,997,000
Capital: Skopje (pop 440,000)
Official language: Macedonian
Religions: Serbian (Macedonian) Orthodox 54%, Islam 30%
Government: Republic
Currency: Denar

YUGOSLAVIA

Area: 102,173 sq km (39,449 sq miles)
Population: 10,614,000
Capital: Belgrade (pop 1,168,000)
Official language: Serbian (Serbo-Croatian)
Religions: Serbian Orthodox 62%, Islam 19%
Government: Republic
Currency: New dinar

Danube The middle course of this important river forms part of the boundary between Croatia and Yugoslavia. It then flows across northern Yugoslavia. Belgrade stands at a point where the Danube joins the Sava, one of its main tributaries.

Marshal Tito (1892-1980) After World War II, Tito (born Josip Broz) served as president of Communist Yugoslavia. He kept the country united. After his death, conflict began between various language and religious groups, which led to a violent breakup of the country.

Ancient Greece was the birthplace of Western civilization. It produced great art and architecture, and influential ideas in government, philosophy and education. Pottery jugs like this one are examples of many beautiful works of art that have survived since ancient times.

Goats can be destructive animals. Herds of them graze on trees and land until they are bare. In southeastern Europe, rain has washed the soil from bare land, causing serious soil erosion.

0   100 miles

0   100 kilometers

Dubrovnik is a beautiful medieval port and resort on the southern coast of Croatia. It was badly shelled during conflict between Croatian and Serbian forces in the 1990s.

Farming is the main economic activity in Albania. Crops include fruits, maize, olives, and wheat. Albania has some mines and factories, but it remains the poorest country in Europe.

botica
Becej
Novi Sad
Danube
Belgrade
Serbia
Kraljevo
Morava
Nis
YUGOSLAVIA
Kosovo
Péc   Pristina
nkodër
Skopje
MACEDONIA
Vardar
Tirana
Bitola
ALBANIA
Kavalla   Alexandroúpolis
Thessalonika   Thasos
Véroia
Mt Olympus
9,626 ft (2917 m)
Limnos
Lárisa
Kérkira
Vólos
Corfu
Aegean Sea
Pindus
Lesbos
Mts
Levkás
Khalkis
Khios
Euboea
Cephalonia   Pátrai
Samos
Athens   Andros
Piraeus
Tinos
Zákinthos
GREECE
Naxos
Kalámai
Kos
Rhodes
Rhodes
MEDITERRANEAN
Khaniá   Iráklion
Crete
SEA

EAST-CENTRAL EUROPE

East-central Europe includes Poland, which faces the Baltic Sea. It also includes the landlocked Czech Republic and Slovakia, which until December 31, 1992, formed a single country, Czechoslovakia.

These countries had Communist governments from 1948 until the early 1990s, when Communist policies were abandoned. In the 1990s, they faced many problems as they restored the land and government-owned industries to private ownership.

POLAND

Area: 323,250 sq km (124,808 sq miles)
Highest point: Rysy Peak 2,499 m (8,199 ft)
Population: 38,650,000
Capital and largest city: Warsaw (pop 1,638,000)
Other large cities: Lódź (825,000)
Krakow (745,000)
Official language: Polish
Religions: Christianity (Roman Catholic 91%, Orthodox and other 9%)
Government: Republic
Currency: Zloty

CZECH REPUBLIC

Area: 78,864 sq km (30,450 sq miles)
Highest point: Snezka, in the Sudeten Mountains, 1,602m (5,256ft)
Population: 10,304,000
Capital and largest city: Prague (pop 1,210,000)
Other large cities: Brno (389,000)
Ostrava (325,000)
Official language: Czech
Religions: Christianity (Roman Catholic 39%)
Government: Republic
Currency: Czech koruna

SLOVAKIA

Area: 49,012 sq km (18,924 sq miles)
Highest point:
Gerlachovsky Stit,2,655 m (8,711 ft)
Population: 5,383,000
Capital and largest city: Bratislava (pop 452,000)
Other large cities: Kosice (241,000)
Presov (93,000)
Official language: Slovak
Religions: Christianity (Roman Catholic 60%)
Government: Republic
Currency: Slovak koruna

Prague, the capital of Czechoslovakia, became the capital of the Czech Republic when Czechoslovakia split apart on January 1, 1993. It is one of the most beautiful cities in eastern Europe.

European bison These animals were once common in Europe, but few now remain. A small herd is protected in the forested Bialowieza National Park, which lies partly in Poland and partly in Belarus.

0 | 100 miles
0 | 100 kilometers

• Gdynia

• **Gdansk** • Elblag

Olsztyn

Elk

Bialystok

Vistula

• Torun

• Wloclawek

Bug

Warsaw
☐

P O L A N D

• **Łódź**

Radom

• Lublin

• Kielce

Czestochowa

Vistula

Katowice

Rzeszów

• Gliwice

• **Kraków**

Przemysl

• Opava

Bielsko-Biala

• Ostrava

C a r p a t h i a n   M t s

Rysy Peak
8,199 ft (2499 m)

▲ *Gerlachovsky Stit*
▲ *8,711 ft (2655 m)* •Presov

•Poprad

Kosice
•

Vah

SLOVAKIA

•Zvolen

• Nitra

Pope John Paul II was born
in Poland. He was elected
Pope in 1978. The Communists
discouraged religious worship,
but many Poles kept their faith
in Catholicism and opposed
Communist rule in their country.

Industry developed rapidly
in Poland and other parts of
eastern Europe under
Communist rule. Factories
powered by coal and oil have
caused severe pollution over
large areas.

Bratislava is the capital of
Slovakia, which was created
on January 1, 1993. Bratislava
stands on the River Danube.
Its factories make chemicals,
machinery, petroleum products,
and textiles.

SOUTHEASTERN EUROPE

Southeastern Europe contains landlocked Hungary and two countries, Romania and Bulgaria, which have coastlines on the Black Sea. All three countries had mainly agricultural economies until they came under Communist rule in the late 1940s. Today manufacturing is the most important activity. In the 1990s, the countries of southeastern Europe faced problems as they worked to restore democracy and private ownership of all economic activity.

HUNGARY

Area: 93,032 sq km (35,920 sq miles)
Highest point: Mount Kekes 1,015 m (3,330 ft)
Population: 10,155,000
Capital and largest city: Budapest (pop 1,885,000)
Other large cities: Debrecen (210,000)
Miskolc (178,000)
Official language: Hungarian
Religions: Christianity (Roman Catholic 63%, Protestant 25%)
Government: Republic
Currency: Forint

ROMANIA

Area: 238,391 sq km (92,043 sq miles)
Highest point: Mount Moldoveanu 2,543 m (8,343 ft)
Population: 22,544,000
Capital and largest city: Bucharest (pop 2,080,000)
Other large cities: Constanta (348,000)
Iasi (340,000)
Official language: Romanian
Religions: Christianity (Romanian Orthodox 87%)
Government: Republic
Currency: Leu

BULGARIA

Area: 110,912 sq km (42,823 sq miles)
Highest point: Musala Peak 2,925 m (9,596 ft)
Population: 8,312,000
Capital and largest city: Sofia (pop 1,117,000)
Other large cities: Plovdiv (344,000)
Varna (301,000)
Official language: Bulgarian
Religions: Christianity (Bulgarian Orthodox 36%), Islam 13%
Government: Republic
Currency: Lev

Wheat is the leading grain crop in southeastern Europe. Maize is also important. Other food crops include fruits, potatoes, sugar beet, and various vegetables.

Budapest, the capital of Hungary, stands on the River Danube River. Tourists visit the city to see its many historic buildings, but Budapest also has many factories, producing such things as chemical products, textiles, and transport equipment.

Wild boars were once common in the forests of central Europe. But most of the original forests have been cut down to make way for farms and cities. Wild boars, along with many other plant and animal species, are now rare.

0   100 miles

0   100 kilometers

Satu Mare

Baja Mare

Botosani

Dej

Iasi

Piatra-Neamt

Cluj-Napoca

Tîrgu Mures

Bacau

R O M A N I A

Carpathian Mts

Prut

Siret

Mures

Sibiu

Hunedoara

Moldoveanu
8,343 ft (2543 m)

Brasov

Galati

Transylvanian Alps

Buzau

Braila

Mouths
of the
Danube

Ploiesti

Pitesti

Craiova

Olt

Bucharest

Danube

Constanta

'idin

Ruse

Dobrich

Balkan Mts

Mikhaylovgrad

Pleven

Varna

Veliko Târnovo

BLACK
SEA

BULGARIA

Sofia

Burgas

Musala Peak
9,596 ft (2925 m)

Stara Zagora

Plovdiv

Blagoevgrad

Dracula, a fictional character, was a vampire who was supposed to have lived in Transylvania, Romania. Legends of vampires may have begun with many brutal murders committed in the 15th century by Vlad Tepes, a prince who ruled in the region.

Tobacco is grown in southeastern Europe, where it flourishes during the warm and sunny summers. Winters are cold but only severe when icy winds blow from the north.

Wine is produced in all three countries in southeastern Europe, and Romania ranks among the world's top ten producers. Many of the wines of this region are now exported to western Europe.

Roses are grown in Bulgaria to make attar of roses. Only the petals of red roses are used to produce this fragrant oil, which is an ingredient of expensive perfumes. A less fragrant attar is made from a white rose.

EASTERN EUROPE

When the Soviet Union broke up in December 1991, following the collapse of Communism, the 15 republics that comprised the Soviet Union became independent nations. The map of eastern Europe shown here contains six of them. In the 1990s, the governments of the new countries worked to set up new democratic political, legal, and economic systems.

Some of these new democratic countries of eastern Europe have applied for membership in the European Community.

 ESTONIA

Area: 45,100 sq km (17,413 sq miles)
Population: 1,458,000
Capital: Tallinn (pop 435,000)
Official language: Estonian
Religions: Christianity 38%
Government: Republic
Currency: Kroon

 LATVIA

Area: 64,600 sq km (24,924 sq miles)
Population: 2,465,000
Capital: Riga (pop 826,000)
Official language: Latvian
Religions: Christianity 40%
Government: Republic
Currency: Lats

 LITHUANIA

Area: 65,200 sq km (25,174 sq miles)
Population: 3,706,000
Capital: Vilnius (pop 573,000)
Official language: Lithuanian
Religions: Christianity (Roman Catholic 72%)
Government: Republic
Currency: Litas

 BELARUS

Area: 207,600 sq km (80,155 sq miles)
Population: 10,267,000
Capital: Minsk (pop 1,695,000)
Official languages: Belarussian, Russian
Religions: Christianity 49%
Government: Republic
Currency: Belarussian rouble

 UKRAINE

Area: 603,700 sq km (233,090 sq miles)
Population: 59,698,000
Capital: Kiev (pop 2,630,000)
Official language: Ukrainian
Religions: Christianity 43%
Government: Republic
Currency: Hryvna

 MOLDOVA

Area: 33,700 sq km (13,012 sq miles)
Population: 4,312,000
Capital: Chisinau (pop 658,000)
Official language: Romanian
Religions: Christianity (Romanian Orthodox 35%)
Government: Republic
Currency: Moldovan leu

Ukraine has been called the breadbasket of Europe because of the amount of wheat it grows on its vast plains. It also ranks as one of the world's top producers of sugar beets. Wheat is grown throughout eastern Europe.

Amber is the hardened resin of ancient pine trees that grew in northern Europe millions of years ago. A large amount is found along the Baltic Sea coasts of Estonia, Latvia, and Lithuania. It is used in jewellery.

0   100 miles

0   100 kilometers

Chernobyl, near Kiev in Ukraine, was the site of the worst nuclear accident in history. An explosion at its nuclear power plant in 1986 released radioactive substances, which were carried by winds into northern and western Europe.

Riga is the capital of Latvia. It stands on the Gulf of Riga and has beautiful medieval buildings. It is also a major industrial city, producing chemicals, electronics, and machinery.

Vitsyebsk

Mahilyow

bruysk

Homyel

Chernobyl

Kiev

Kharkov

U K R A I N E

Poltava

Kramatorsk

Luhansk

Horlivka

Dneprodzerzinsk

Dnepropetrovsk

Makiyivka

Kryvyy Rih

Zaporozje

Donetsk

Mariupol'

Kherson

Dnepr

Melitopol

Odessa

Sea of Azov

Simferopol'

Sevastopol

Black Sea

Wolves, which are one of the ancestors of domestic dogs, are found throughout eastern Europe. They live mostly in open country where there is cover. Their numbers have been greatly reduced by hunting.

Flax is a leading crop in Belarus and Ukraine. These two countries are among the world's top ten producers. Flax fiber is used to make linen, and the seeds to make linseed oil.

EUROPEAN RUSSIA

Only part of Russia, the world's largest country, is in Europe. The rest is in Asia. Russia had a troubled history in the 20th century. In 1917, Communists took power. From 1922, Russia became part of a vast country called the Soviet Union. In World War II (1939-45), German forces invaded European Russia and caused great destruction. In 1991, the Soviet Union broke up into 15 countries. The largest of these is Russia.

RUSSIA

Area: 17,075.400 sq km (6,592,850 sq miles), of which about 25% is in Europe
Highest point: Mount Elbrus, in the Caucasus Mountains, 5,642 m (18,510 ft)
Population: 147,307,000 (about 80% of whom live in European Russia)
Capital and largest city: Moscow (pop 8,400,000)
Other large cities (in European Russia):
St Petersburg (4,200,000)
Nizhny Novgorod (1,400,000)
Samara (1,200,000)
Kazan (1,100,000)
Official language: Russian
Religions: Christianity (Russian Orthodox 16%), Islam 10%
Government: Republic
Currency: Rouble

ASIAN RUSSIA
Asian Russia is thinly populated. Though three-quarters of Russia is in Asia, it contains only 20 percent of Russia's people.

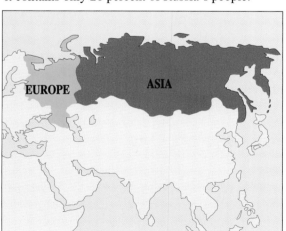

Hammer and sickle
This Communist symbol appeared in gold on the red flag that was used by the former Soviet Union. It represented the nation's industrial and agricultural workers.

Vladimir Lenin (1870-1924) founded the Russian Communist Party and led the revolution in 1917 that made Russia a Communist country.

Icons are religious paintings found in Eastern Orthodox churches. The Communists discouraged religious worship, but Christianity survived. The Russian Orthodox Church is the largest religious denomination in Russia.

Murmansk

Lake Onega

Lake Ladoga

Gulf of Finland

St Petersburg

Cherepove

Novgorod

Moscow

Kaluga

Tu

Smolensk

0	200 miles
0	200 kilometers

Sea of Azov

Blac

Ballet is one of Russia's major art forms. The Kirov Ballet of St Petersburg and the Bolshoi Theatre Ballet in Moscow are world famous. Russian composers include Nikolai Rimsky-Korsakov, Peter Ilich Tchaikovsky, and Igor Stravinsky.

Barents Sea

Vorkuta •

• Archangel'sk

Ukhta •

Northern Dvina

• Kotlas

Pechora

Ural Mountains

R U S S I A

• Vologda

Kirov

Perm

Izhevsk

Yaroslavl

**Nizhniy
Novgorod**   **Kazan**   *Kama*

Volga

Ufa

• Ryazan

Magnitogorsk

Samara

Penza   Syzran

Orenburg

• Saratov

Ural

Voronezh

Don

• **Volgograd**

Volga

• Rostov

Astrakhan

rasnodar • Stavrapol'

Caspian Sea

Sochi

Grozny

C a u c a s u s

*Mt Elbrus
18,510 ft
(5642 m)*

Machachkala

Sea

Kremlin This ancient fortress
in Moscow is Russia's seat of
government. The Kremlin also
contains many beautiful
buildings that are now
museums.

Brown bears live in the
northern forests of European
Russia. Hunting for furs has
greatly reduced the number
of wild animals in Russia, but
many species are now
protected in nature reserves.

Industry Russia's many resources
include coal, oil, and many
metals. The country has
many heavy industries,
which, under
Communism, were
owned by the
government. In the
1990s, Russia
worked to restore
private ownership
of the land and
industry.

ПЬЗЖ

Cyrillic alphabet Russian is written
in the Cyrillic alphabet, which was
invented in the 9th century by two
Greek missionaries, St Cyril and his
brother, St Methodius.

PEOPLE AND BELIEFS

Europe is the home of about 12.5 percent of the world's population. It ranks third among the continents in population, after Asia and Africa, which overtook it in the late 1990s. Large parts of northern Europe contain few people, but the central plains of Europe and the Mediterranean region contain some of the most densely populated areas in the world. Many people live in huge cities. Europe's largest cities include Paris, Moscow, London, Berlin, and Athens.

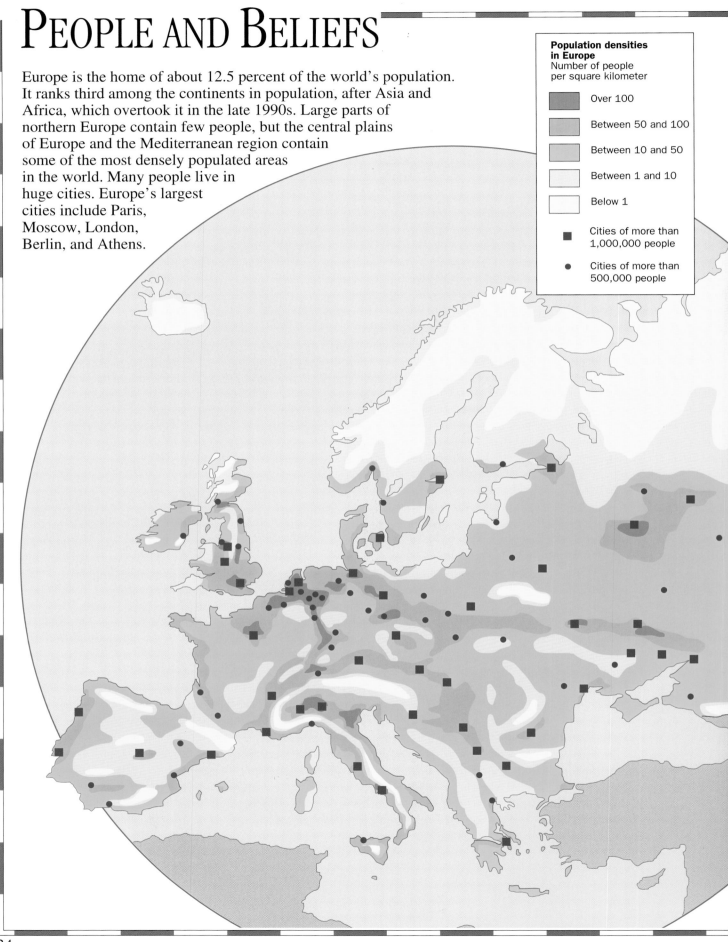

Population densities in Europe
Number of people per square kilometer

- Over 100
- Between 50 and 100
- Between 10 and 50
- Between 1 and 10
- Below 1
- ■ Cities of more than 1,000,000 people
- • Cities of more than 500,000 people

Population and Area

Although only 25 percent of Russia lies in Europe, it is by far the largest country in Europe both in area and in population. Ukraine, another country created in 1991 when the Soviet Union broke up, is the second-largest country, although in population it ranks sixth.

Germany has the second-largest population in Europe, although it ranks only sixth in area. The third most populous European country is the much smaller United Kingdom, which ranks eleventh in area.

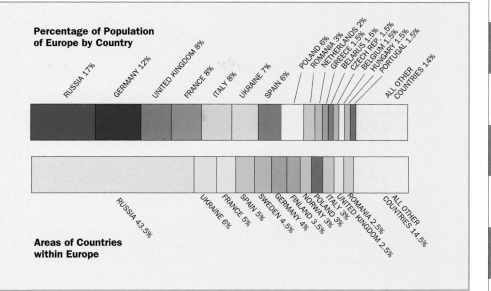

Percentage of Population of Europe by Country

RUSSIA 17% · GERMANY 12% · UNITED KINGDOM 8% · FRANCE 8% · ITALY 8% · UKRAINE 7% · SPAIN 6% · POLAND 6% · ROMANIA 3% · NETHERLANDS 2% · GREECE 1.5% · BELARUS 1.5% · CZECH REP. 1.5% · BELGIUM 1.5% · HUNGARY 1.5% · PORTUGAL 1.5% · ALL OTHER COUNTRIES 14%

RUSSIA 43.5% · UKRAINE 6% · FRANCE 5% · SPAIN 5% · SWEDEN 4.5% · GERMANY 4% · FINLAND 3.5% · NORWAY 3% · POLAND 3% · ITALY 3% · UNITED KINGDOM 2.5% · ROMANIA 2.5% · ALL OTHER COUNTRIES 14.5%

Areas of Countries within Europe

Main religious groups

Christianity, the main religion in Europe, has played an important part in the continent's history, and the great Christian cathedrals testify to its influence on art and architecture.

Roman Catholics make up the largest single group. Governed from Rome, they are strongest in southern Europe and parts of eastern Europe, especially Poland. The other main Christian groups are Orthodox Christians and the Protestants. Orthodox Christians live chiefly in Greece, the southern nations in eastern Europe, and Russia. Protestants are most numerous in the northern countries of western Europe. Europe also has Jewish and Islamic communities. Jews live in most parts of Europe, while Muslims live in the Balkans and also in countries, such as France and Germany, that have large numbers of immigrants from North Africa and the Middle East.

Many people in eastern Europe and elsewhere in Europe do not follow any established religion.

Legend:
- Roman Catholic
- Orthodox
- Orthodox and Islamic
- Protestant
- Protestant and Roman Catholic

The great medieval cathedrals of Europe are architectural masterpieces that contain priceless works of art. Thousands of people visit them every year.

CLIMATE AND VEGETATION

Europe's climates range from polar and tundra in the northeast to Mediterranean in the south. The northwest has a mild climate, because temperatures are raised by a warm offshore current, called the North Atlantic Drift – the northern part of the Gulf Stream, which starts in the Gulf of Mexico. Northern Europe has large cold forests of coniferous trees. The natural vegetation of most of central Europe was deciduous forest, with trees that shed their leaves in autumn. Most of this deciduous forest has been cut down to create farmland and space for cities.

Europe's Natural Vegetation

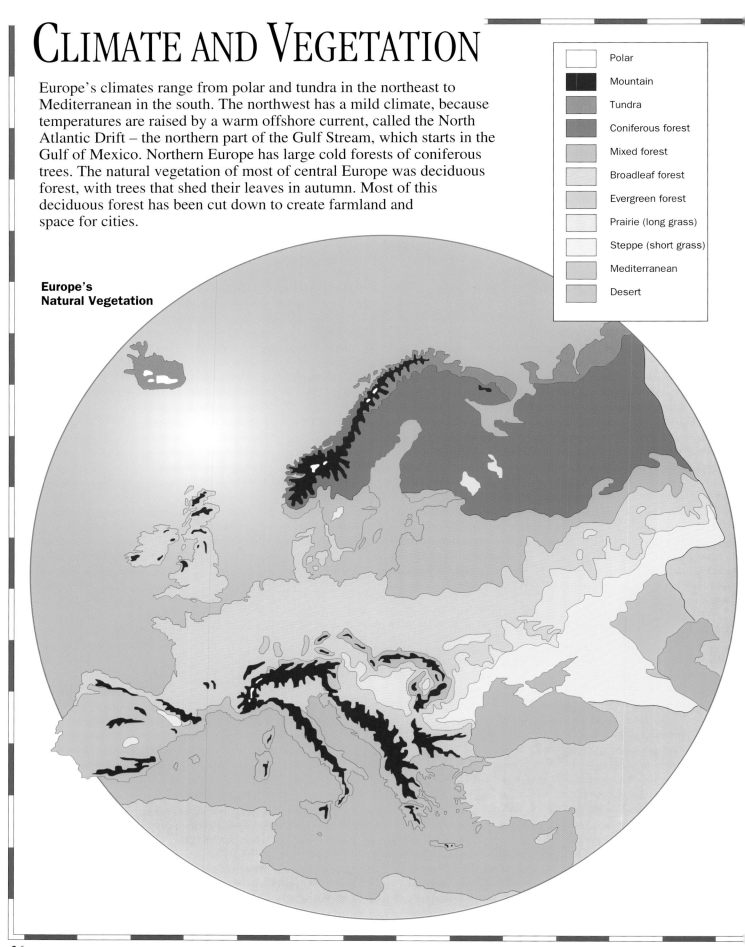

Polar

Mountain

Tundra

Coniferous forest

Mixed forest

Broadleaf forest

Evergreen forest

Prairie (long grass)

Steppe (short grass)

Mediterranean

Desert

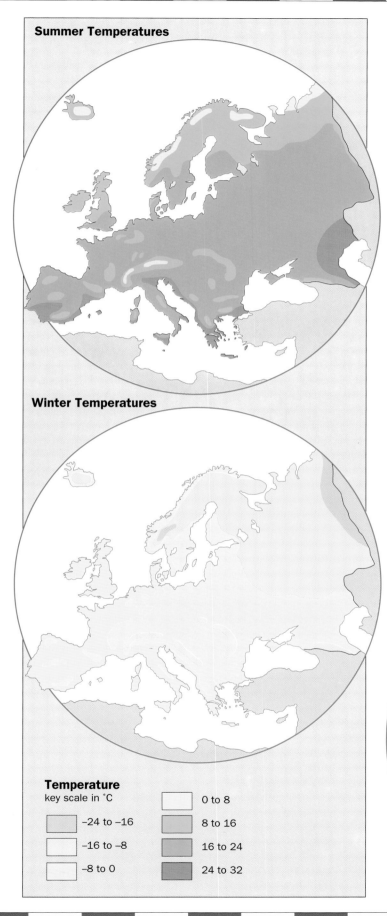

Summer Temperatures

Winter Temperatures

Range of Climates

Europe's climate varies from the cold north to the temperate south. The climate also changes from west to east. In the west, the climate is influenced by the Atlantic Ocean. The ocean makes summers milder and winters warmer. To the east, the climate becomes more extreme, with hotter summers and bitterly cold winters. Rainfall in eastern Europe is generally less than in the west.

Ranges of Vegetation

The three main types of vegetation in Europe are treeless tundra, forests, and grasslands. (Mountains, which get colder with altitude, also have these three types of vegetation.) In the coldest northern regions, summers are short. When the topsoil thaws, low plants grow, providing food for herds of reindeer and other animals. The northern forests contain coniferous trees that can survive the cold winters. Farther south are mixed forests of evergreen and deciduous trees. Central and southern Europe have broadleaf forests, containing ash, birch, beech, maple, and oak. In the Mediterranean, many trees, including pines, cork oaks, and olives, have tough leaves that retain moisture during the hot summers and stay on the trees all year. Grasslands occur in regions with dry climates. The best-known grasslands are in Ukraine and southern Russia. They are called the steppes.

Annual rainfall
in mm

	Above 1500
	1000 - 1500
	750 - 1000
	500 - 750
	0 - 500

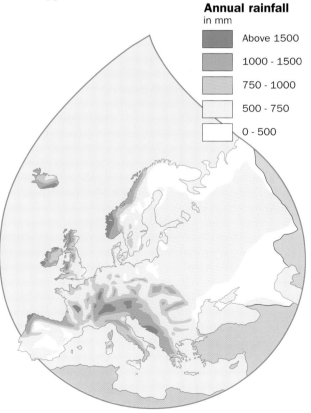

Temperature
key scale in °C

−24 to −16	0 to 8
−16 to −8	8 to 16
−8 to 0	16 to 24
	24 to 32

ECOLOGY AND ENVIRONMENT

Europe is a prosperous continent, but economic development has caused great damage to the environment. Farming has destroyed natural habitats, harming wildlife. Industry has also caused pollution – in the air, rivers and seas, and also on land. Pollution from one country often spreads to others. Today, the governments of most European countries are working to prevent further damage.

Seals have suffered greatly in recent years from oil spills and the dumping of toxic wastes.

ICELAND

NORWAY

FINLAND

SWEDEN

ESTONIA

LATVIA

DENMARK

LITHUANIA

KALININGRAD (RUSSIA)

RUSSIA

IRELAND

UNITED KINGDOM

Oil spill

NETHERLANDS

Flood

BELARUS

POLAND

Oil spill

GERMANY

BELGIUM

LUXEMBOURG

CZECH REP.

Nuclear accident

FRANCE

SLOVAKIA

UKRAINE

SWITZERLAND

AUSTRIA

HUNGARY

MOLDOVA

Flood

SLOVENIA

ROMANIA

Flood

CROATIA

SPAIN

ANDORRA

BOSNIA & HERZEGOVINA

PORTUGAL

ITALY

YUGOSLAVIA

BULGARIA

MACEDONIA

ALBANIA

Earthquake

GREECE

Earthquake

MALTA

Environmental Damage to Land and Sea

Area affected by acid rain	▼ Sea dumping sites
Area at risk of desertification	● Worst urban polluters
Most polluted seas	● Major environmental disasters and type
Most polluted rivers	

Natural Hazards

Volcanic eruptions occur in southern Italy and Iceland, while earthquakes affect some areas, especially the eastern Mediterranean. Global warming caused by air pollution has begun to change weather patterns. Unusual weather, such as exceptionally heavy rains and storms, has caused severe floods in some areas, such as France.

Damaging the Environment

The use of smokeless fuels has greatly reduced air pollution in many European cities, but factories, power stations, and motor vehicles still pump poisonous gases into the air. These gases are dissolved by water droplets in the air and return to the ground as acid rain. The chemicals kill trees and wildlife in rivers and lakes. Air pollution has also caused global warming and damage to the ozone layer, which protects us from the sun's harmful ultraviolet radiation.

Intensive farming in dry areas, such as southeastern Spain, has turned once fertile land into barren desert. Industrial and agricultural wastes have polluted rivers, while oil spills from tankers have greatly harmed marine life.

Accidents at nuclear power stations release dangerous nuclear fallout. Europe's worst nuclear accident occurred when explosions and fire damaged a nuclear power plant at Chernobyl, Ukraine, in 1986.

Diseases and Deaths

The leading causes of death in western Europe are circulatory diseases (which cause heart attacks and strokes), cancer, and car accidents.

Number of deaths each year from cancer per 100,000 people

| 200 | 225 | 250 | 275 | 300 + |

Number of deaths each year from heart disease per 100,000 people

| 100 | 150 | 200 | 250 | 300 + |

Number of deaths each year from road traffic accidents per 100,000 people

| 10 | 15 | 20 | 25 | 30 + |

Eastern European figures not available

Endangered Species

During the Ice Age, many species became extinct as the ice sheets advanced and retreated. However, since the end of the Ice Age, about 10,000 years ago, the land has been transformed into a patchwork of farms and towns. The destruction of habitats has led to some extinctions, while many animals have disappeared from areas that they once inhabited.

Hunting for food and skins, and the slaughter of animals such as bears and wolves to protect domestic animals, have also reduced the ranges of many creatures. Pressures on wildlife remain as the continuing destruction of hedgerows, land reclamation, military exercises, and the growth of tourism continue to reduce natural habitats.

Ladies-slipper orchid

Some Endangered Species in Europe

Birds and Butterflies
Dalmatian pelican
Golden eagle
Swallowtail butterfly

Mammals
European bison
Horseshoe bat
Ibex
Lynx
Otter

Marine Mammals
Common seal
Loggerhead turtle

Trees and Plants
Bog pimpernel
Dwarf birch
Irish spurge
Ladies-slipper orchid

ECONOMY

Most European countries are highly developed. They produce large amounts of manufactured goods and farm products but have to import food and many raw materials for their industries. Trade is very important to Europe's economy.

To increase trade and to encourage economic growth, 15 countries – Austria, Belgium, Denmark, Finland, France, Germany, Greece, the Republic of Ireland, Italy, Luxembourg, the Netherlands, Portugal, Spain, Sweden, and the United Kingdom belong to the European Union, and 11 of the nations share a new currency called the Euro. Until the late 1980s, the economies of the Communist countries in eastern Europe were run by their governments. In the 1990s, these countries worked to increase private ownership.

The Wealth of Europe Comes From

✈ Aviation	🍃 Gas	🛢 Oil	☂ Tourism
🧶 Cotton	💻 High-tech industries	🫒 Olive oil	🌾 Wheat
🐟 Fishing	🐄 Livestock	🐑 Sheep/wool	🍇 Wines
🌲 Forest products	🏭 Manufacturing	🚬 Tobacco	
🍇 Fruits	⛏ Mining and minerals		

Gross National Product

In order to compare the economies of countries, experts work out the gross national product (GNP) of the countries in United States dollars. The GNP is the total value of the goods and services produced by a country in a year. The chart, right, shows that the countries with the highest GNPs in 1997 were Germany, France, the United Kingdom, and Italy. The combined GNP of the 15 members of the European Union is one-tenth larger than that of the United States.

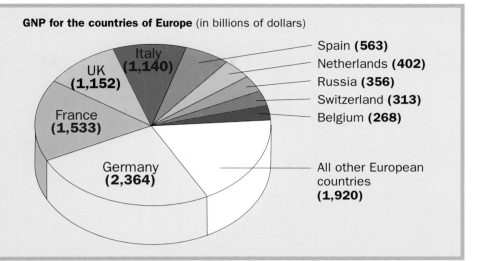

GNP for the countries of Europe (in billions of dollars)

Italy (1,140)
UK (1,152)
France (1,533)
Germany (2,364)
Spain (563)
Netherlands (402)
Russia (356)
Switzerland (313)
Belgium (268)
All other European countries (1,920)

Sources of Energy

Coal and hydroelectricity were once the chief sources of power in Europe. Major coal producers are Russia, Ukraine, and Poland. Hydroelectricity is important in rainy, mountainous countries, such as Norway.

Today, oil and natural gas have become major sources of power, while coal has become less important. Europe's oil producers include Britain and Norway, which share the oilfields in the North Sea, and Russia. Leading natural gas producers include Britain, the Netherlands, Norway, and Russia. Major nuclear power-producing countries include France, Germany, and Russia. Other sources of energy, including solar, wind, and wave power, are now being developed in Europe.

Per Capita GNPs

Per capita means per head or per person. Per capita GNPs are worked out by dividing the GNP by the population. For example, the per capita GNP of the oil-rich country of Norway is US $36,100. By contrast, Albania has a per capita GNP of only $760, which places it among the world's poorest countries.

Sources of energy found in Europe

- 🛢 Oil
- 💧 Gas
- ≋ Hydroelectricity
- ⚒ Coal
- ☢ Uranium

POLITICS AND HISTORY

Between the late 1940s and the 1980s, the democratic countries of the West were opposed to the Communist countries in the east. This conflict was called the Cold War. In the 1980s, the collapse of Communism in the Soviet Union and eastern Europe rearranged Europe's map. In the 1990s, the West helped the former Communist countries rebuild their economies. The Cold War was over, but new conflicts arose. In particular, civil wars occurred when rival ethnic and religious groups fought for power in Chechnya, Russia, and in former Yugoslavia.

The Romans dominated Europe with their army. Foot soldiers regularly marched vast distances carrying equipment weighing more than 40 kg (88 lb).

Great Events
After the end of the Ice Age, about 10,000 years ago, the warm climate led to a rapid growth in the human population of Europe. Around 5,000 years ago, civilizations began to develop in the eastern Mediterranean. Between 500 and 300 BC, the ancient Greek civilization reached its peak. It was succeeded by the Roman Empire, which developed art, learning and commerce.

Following the fall of the Roman Empire, Europe declined. The early 14th century, however, saw the beginning of a period, known for its brilliant art and a revival of learning, called the Renaissance. Towards the end of this period, in the 15th and 16th centuries, Europeans began to found overseas colonies.

The Industrial Revolution began in Europe in the late 18th century. In the late 19th century, Europeans colonized much of the world. The 20th century saw two major world wars and frequent changes to the map of Europe. The century ended with the hope that international cooperation could prevent future continental wars.

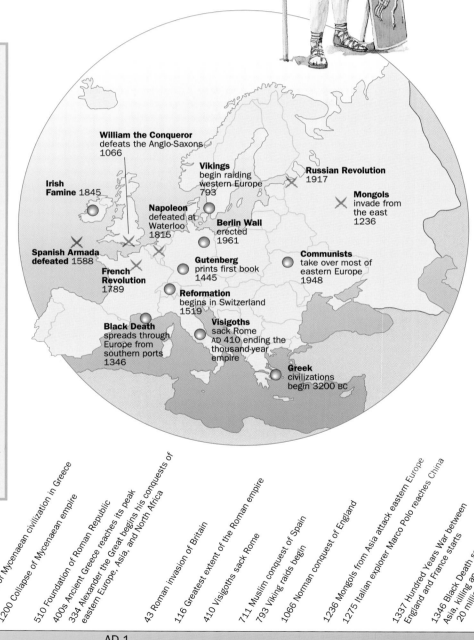

William the Conqueror defeats the Anglo-Saxons 1066

Vikings begin raiding western Europe 793

Russian Revolution 1917

Mongols invade from the east 1236

Irish Famine 1845

Napoleon defeated at Waterloo 1815

Berlin Wall erected 1961

Spanish Armada defeated 1588

Communists take over most of eastern Europe 1948

Gutenberg prints first book 1445

French Revolution 1789

Reformation begins in Switzerland 1519

Black Death spreads through Europe from southern ports 1346

Visigoths sack Rome AD 410 ending the thousand-year empire

Greek civilizations begin 3200 BC

20,000 Evidence of cave dwellers in various sites throughout Europe

6500 Farming in Greece

3200 Early Cycladic civilization in Aegean Sea

1600 Rise of Mycenaean civilization in Greece

1200 Collapse of Mycenaean empire

510 Foundation of Roman Republic

400s Ancient Greece reaches its peak

334 Alexander the Great begins his conquests of eastern Europe, Asia, and North Africa

43 Roman invasion of Britain

116 Greatest extent of the Roman empire

410 Visigoths sack Rome

711 Muslim conquest of Spain

793 Viking raids begin

1066 Norman conquest of England

1236 Mongols from Asia attack eastern Europe

1275 Italian explorer Marco Polo reaches China

1337 Hundred Years War between England and France starts

1346 Black Death spreads from Asia, killing an estimated 20 million Europeans

20,000 BC   AD 1

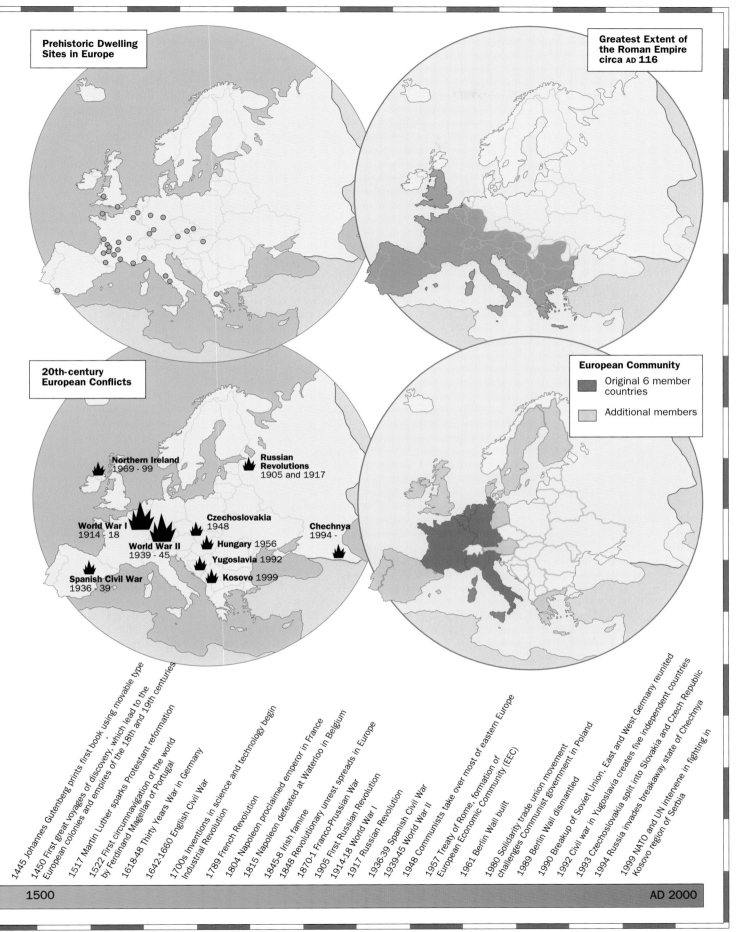

Prehistoric Dwelling Sites in Europe

Greatest Extent of the Roman Empire circa AD 116

20th-century European Conflicts

Northern Ireland
1969 - 99

Russian
Revolutions
1905 and 1917

World War I
1914 - 18

Czechoslovakia
1948

Chechnya
1994 -

World War II
1939 - 45

Hungary 1956

Yugoslavia 1992

Spanish Civil War
1936 - 39

Kosovo 1999

European Community

Original 6 member countries

Additional members

1445 Johannes Gutenberg prints first book using movable type

1450 First great voyages of discovery, which lead to the European colonies and empires of the 18th and 19th centuries

1517 Martin Luther sparks Protestant reformation

1522 First circumnavigation of the world by Ferdinand Magellan of Portugal

1618-48 Thirty Years War in Germany

1642-1660 English Civil War

1700s Inventions in science and technology begin Industrial Revolution

1789 French Revolution

1804 Napoleon proclaimed emperor in France

1815 Napoleon defeated at Waterloo in Belgium

1845-8 Irish famine

1848 Revolutionary unrest spreads in Europe

1870-1 Franco-Prussian War

1905 First Russian Revolution

1914-18 World War I

1917 Russian Revolution

1936-39 Spanish Civil War

1939-45 World War II

1948 Communists take over most of eastern Europe

1957 Treaty of Rome, formation of European Economic Community (EEC)

1961 Berlin Wall built

1980 Solidarity trade union movement challenges Communist government in Poland

1989 Berlin Wall dismantled

1990 Breakup of Soviet Union, East and West Germany reunited

1992 Civil war in Yugoslavia creates five independent countries

1993 Czechoslovakia split into Slovakia and Czech Republic

1994 Russia invades breakaway state of Chechnya

1999 NATO and UN intervene in fighting in Kosovo region of Serbia

1500

AD 2000

ATLANTIC OCEAN

The Atlantic is the world's second-largest ocean, after the Pacific. It stretches from the Arctic Ocean in the North to the icy continent of Antarctica around the South Pole. Greenland is the largest of the many islands in the Atlantic Ocean.

Strong currents move through the Atlantic. The warm Gulf Stream starts in the Gulf of Mexico and flows northeast to Europe. It warms coastal areas in northwest Europe. By contrast, the icy Labrador current flows south from the Arctic and chills the northeastern coasts of North America.

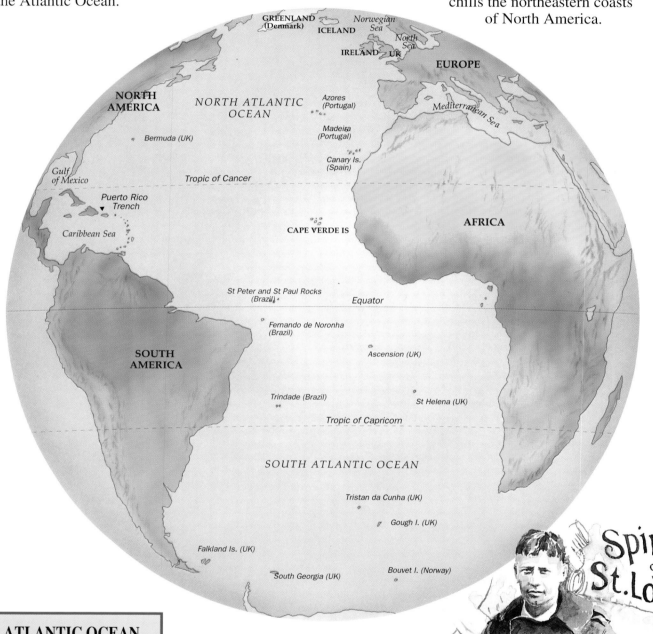

GREENLAND (Denmark)
Norwegian Sea
ICELAND
North Sea
IRELAND UK
EUROPE

NORTH AMERICA
NORTH ATLANTIC OCEAN
Azores (Portugal)
Mediterranean Sea

Bermuda (UK)
Madeira (Portugal)
Canary Is. (Spain)

Gulf of Mexico
Tropic of Cancer

Puerto Rico Trench
Caribbean Sea
CAPE VERDE IS
AFRICA

St Peter and St Paul Rocks (Brazil)
Equator

Fernando de Noronha (Brazil)
Ascension (UK)

SOUTH AMERICA
Trindade (Brazil)
St Helena (UK)
Tropic of Capricorn

SOUTH ATLANTIC OCEAN

Tristan da Cunha (UK)
Gough I. (UK)
Falkland Is. (UK)
Bouvet I. (Norway)
South Georgia (UK)

Spirit of St. Louis

ATLANTIC OCEAN
Area: about 106,000,000 sq km (41,000,000 sq miles)
Average depth: 3,580 m (about 11,700 ft)
Deepest point: Milwaukee Deep, in the Puerto Rico Trench, 8,648 m (28,374 ft)

Charles Lindbergh (1902-74), an American aviator, made the first solo non-stop flight across the Atlantic Ocean in May 1927. Today the ocean is a busy highway and is extremely important in world trade.

ARCTIC OCEAN

The Arctic is the smallest of the world's four oceans. It is bordered by North America, Asia, and northwestern Europe. It is linked to the Atlantic by the broad Norwegian Sea. The North Pole lies near its centre.

Sea ice covers much of the Arctic Ocean, and this stopped early explorers from finding a sea passage that would be a short cut from Europe to the Far East. They searched for a northeast passage north of Asia and a northwest passage north of North America. The first voyage through the Northeast Passage around Asia took place in 1878-9 and the first through the Northwest Passage was first completed in 1906. Neither route was good for trade.

PACIFIC OCEAN

Bering Sea

60°

Arctic Circle

70°

Permanent pack ice

Beaufort Sea

80°

180°

NORTH AMERICA

Laptev Sea

ASIA

120°

120°

ARCTIC OCEAN

North Pole

Severnaya Zemlya (Russia)

Hudson Bay

Ellesmere I.

60°

Kara Sea

Baffin Bay

60°

Franz Josef Land (Russia)

Novaya Zemlya (Russia)

0°

Svalbard (Norway)

GREENLAND (Denmark)

Greenland Sea

Barents Sea

Labrador Sea

Limit of Winter pack ice

Norwegian Sea

ICELAND

ATLANTIC OCEAN

EUROPE

Robert E Peary (1856-1920), a US Navy Commander, was the first explorer to reach the North Pole. He crossed the sea ice with his assistant Matthew Henson and four Inuits, reaching the Pole on April 6, 1909.

ARCTIC OCEAN

Area: about 13,230,000 sq km (5,110,000 sq miles)
Average depth: 1,120 m (about 3,670 ft)
Deepest point: about 5,550 m (18,044 ft) north of Svalbard

INDEX

Picture credits
Photographs: British Airways 11
EEC 4
The Hutchison Library 5, 11, 15, 19, 26, 27, 28, 31
Travel Photo International 5, 6, 12, 23, 25, 33, 35